Miracles

By STUART WILDE

Books:

The Taos Quintet:
Miracles
The Force
Affirmations
The Quickening
The Trick to Money Is Having Some!

〜 〜 〜

Infinite Self: 33 Steps to Reclaiming Your Inner Power
"Life Was Never Meant to Be a Struggle"
The Little Money Bible
The Secrets of Life
Silent Powe
Simply Wilde
Sixth Sense
Weight Loss for the Mind
Whispering Winds of Change

〜 〜 〜

Audiocassettes:

The Art of Meditation
The Force (audio book)
Happiness Is Your Destiny
Intuition
Loving Relationships
Miracles (audio book)
Silent Power (audio book)

Available at your local bookstore, or call Hay House, Inc.:
(800) 654-5126

Please visit the Hay House Website at:
hayhouse.com and
Stuart's Website at:
powersource.com/wilde

Miracles

Stuart Wilde

Hay House, Inc.
Carlsbad, California • Sydney, Australia

Published and distributed in the United States by:

Hay House, Inc., P.O. Box 5100
Carlsbad, CA 92018-5100
(800) 654-5126 • Fax: (800) 650-5115

Book design: Highpoint Graphics, Claremont, CA

Library of Congress Cataloging-in-Publication Data

Wilde, Stuart.
    Miracles / Stuart Wilde. —Rev. ed.
      p.   cm.
    ISBN 1-56170-540-3 (tradepaper)
    1. Success—Miscellanea. 2. Miracles. 3. Occultism. I. Title.
BF1999.W5584 1998
131—dc21   97-53047
                                                CIP

ISBN 1–56170–540–3

03 02 01 00   14 13 12 11

First Published in 1983 by Nacson & Sons, Pty., Sydney, Australia
12th printing, 1987
1st printing, Revised Edition, 1988

11th Printing, Revised Edition, April 2000, by Hay House, Inc.

Printed in Canada

CONTENTS ∽

MIRACLES

Creating miracles in your life is no more complicated than understanding the metaphysics of the Universal Law. And because that law is indestructible and therefore infinite, we know that the power used by miracle-makers in the past is still available today. Yet, in our modern society, we are brought up to believe only in those things we can logically understand. We are not taught either that the Universal Law has limitless potential or that this power is at our disposal and can be used to work miracles in our own lives.

STEP ONE ❧

Understanding the Universal Law

To understand miracles, we have to look at two aspects of the Universal Law. First, there lies deep within all mankind an immense power, and second, the power is impartial and unemotional. Call it the Universal Mind, or Christ Consciousness, or what you will, it is this power that allows man a recognition of the universal life force that we call "God."

1

The life force is eternal and universal, and, because of its limitless capacity, it is a part of all things. Moreover, it is a major part of each of us. Consequently, we all have within us an *unlimited power*. Creating miracles in our lives becomes a matter of identifying with the power, understanding its characteristics, and learning to use it effectively. This identification is achieved by knowing that the power is within you and acknowledging that fact by saying, "I am eternal, immortal, universal, and infinite, and what I am is beautiful." In this manner, you lock into the power source and you are poised for the next step, which involves looking at its characteristics.

The Universal Law is impartial and unemotional. It has no way of knowing what you want, nor does it discriminate between your hopes and aspirations, likes and dislikes—it is pure energy. It accepts whatever thoughts, feelings, and actions you project and reflects them back to you unemotionally in the form of events that you experience day to day.

In much the same way that electricity illuminates both a brothel and the vicar's tea party, the Universal Law does not differentiate between different types of energy in your life. It will give you anything you believe in—no more and no less. Therefore, the key to understanding miracles is to look at the beliefs you express as thoughts and feelings.

When you are born, your thoughts and feelings are limitless because your mind is a clean slate. What a small child projects to the Universal Law is a natural purity unbounded by the constraints of beliefs. Children often attempt the seemingly impossible: Unaware that they have any physical limitations, they drive off in the family car or walk on a high ledge. It is only later, through education, that they learn the confines of human expectancy.

But these confines or boundaries are illusions. They are formed by belief patterns, most of them born of ignorance, handed down from generation to generation. This pool of belief patterns or "collective unconscious," as Carl Jung called it, gains validity as it moves through time, and eventually the concepts that later generations experience as physical reality become rigid and domineering. It is as if billions of people who preceded you have determined what you are going to experience on the earth plane, and that is all there is to it.

This rigidity does not allow for genius or for the understanding that we are now in an era of rapid unfoldment. Fundamental structures are being swept away in an avalanche of awareness, and we are no longer prepared just to read about great miracle-makers; we want to have the same experience. For most people, this is not possible because they are locked within the limitations of body and mind; their upbringing is so dominant that it encases their entire evolution, and they experience little spiritual growth.

STEP TWO ᕬ

Understanding
Life's
Mission

We are not our bodies or our emotions or our minds or any of the structures and restrictions we experience around us. We are an infinite part of the God-Force, using the physical form to experience spiritual development through a special teaching called "daily life."

When you entered the earth plane, the energy that is the real you left its abode in the higher dimensions of pure light and entered, by choice, the body you are now in. You chose the circumstances of this life because it was the next step in your infinite evolution, and because this life would allow you to expand what you are spiritually so that you could become an even greater expression of the infinite life force or Living Spirit.

Now, you may say: "That's nuts. Why would I choose these circumstances of my life, this family, this society, and this neighborhood? Why did I not choose a more affluent environment or prettier body or more intellectual capacity?" The answer lies in a dimension beyond the physical plane. As you entered this dimension through birth, you had within your consciousness a heroic mission—a goal. The nature of that goal is firmly written in the very deepest recesses of the inner you, and what you are today, no matter what you feel about yourself, is actually a part of that goal in various stages of completion.

Your mind began recording events, thoughts, and feelings only at birth. It does not know of your heroic mission nor does it understand the Universal Law that interacts with your limitless potential. Why? Two reasons: First, if your mind, feelings, and emotions knew the nature of your heroic goal in life, there would be no challenge or quest, and your evolution would suffer. Second, most understanding of metaphysics is based on tribal or religious beliefs that do not totally reflect an accurate perception of the delicacy of energy and the way its ebb and flow affects daily life; no real understanding of the Universal Law has ever been incorporated into the various belief patterns of the world's collective unconscious.

For example, let us say that your heroic goal in life is to learn to love yourself
and to accept full cosmic responsibility for
what you are. And, let us say, you have
had a number of previous experiences on
the earth plane in which you were weak
and indulged yourself metaphysically by
leaning on others rather than contributing
to your own energy or support. If you
knew this in advance, you would begin to
favor one course of action over another.
You would intellectualize yourself into
positions or feelings that you wanted to
achieve, and your mind would dominate
your every move. Evolution does not
work that way. You cannot overcome
weakness by fighting it or thinking your
way out of it. You overcome weakness by
leaving it behind you. This means that
you become aware of the inner tendencies
that bring you down, that do not support

a belief in self, that do not endorse a love of self, and you say, "I don't want to be that anymore." You then move yourself out of the slovenly ways of the collective unconscious, into a discipline of power. From time to time, you may drift back, but once you decide on the side of strength, the power of the Universal Law will always be with you to varying degrees.

It may be a battle at first, because your mind does not understand these laws or the nature of your mission on earth, nor does it understand the laws that govern your potential. It will have a tendency to "advise" you logically from its own experience, and logic is death to that part of you that is the miracle-maker.

❧ ❧ ❧

Understanding the Nature of Beliefs

The next step in creating your own miracles is to look at the nature of beliefs. By reviewing beliefs and feelings, you begin to understand how to use the Universal Law effectively. It is natural to yearn for the impossible, and in so doing, you establish strong beliefs about what can be done and what cannot. You can jump a certain height and no higher, run at a certain speed and no faster, accept a certain position and no better.

Because most commercial aircraft fly at about 600 miles an hour, the shortest time in which you can get from New York to Paris is about six hours. Those are facts in the collective unconscious. But what if we told you of a man who could move his body many thousands of miles in just a few seconds? Your mind would scan its memory banks and draw a blank, whereupon you might think, *impossible*. Then perhaps you might review all the scientific data available and conclude that this feat is unachievable. All scientific knowledge and current thinking are products of the same collective unconscious, and just the fact that a billion people have no concept of a man moving three thousand miles in a few seconds makes it impossible. But the billions of people are wrong.

There is a dimension, right here on the earth plane, in which such a feat is possible, and there are a few people alive today who know of this dimension and use it. It is a matter of perception and belief. Your ability to work miracles is predicated entirely on how easily and quickly you can give the collective unconscious the slip. It is your attachment to the collective unconscious, or world belief patterns, that holds you back.

This attachment, which you accepted at birth, is your main challenge in life, and your spiritual goal is to step above it. Eventually, you realize that, in order to become part of a higher consciousness, you have to leave where you are right now and step into the unknown. That is why all the tales of the path of the initiate talk about loneliness, for as you move away from old energy, there is a sense of loss.

As you take that step, your perceptions expand gradually to accept a higher vibration of self, and you understand that what others believe is a part of their evolution, but it is not the sum total of all the facts. We experience life through the five senses, "the windows of the soul," and we are taught what capacity those senses have. Yet, each of them has a dimension that is many times deeper than is normally perceived, and those dimensions will open for you as you move toward them.

Let us look at feelings. Through feelings, you can enter into other worlds, and clairsentiousness (a heightened sense of feelings) is a capacity you can learn to develop quite quickly. It is not as acute as extrasensory sight, but it is deep, and through it, you enter into areas of perception that few people ever experience.

Everything around you is energy—your body, its various organs, your thoughts, the physical place you inhabit, the events of your life—each expresses an energy. A part of that energy is perceivable through the five senses, but most of it is beyond normal perception. By opening to the power of the Universal Law and controlling the mind through centering and discipline, you become aware of the subtlety of energies around you. You will find that you can use your feelings to guide you through life. As you move into a situation, push your feeling into whatever lies ahead. How does it feel? What is the Universal Law saying to you? Which area flows, and which does not? After a while, this exercise becomes simple and very accurate. You may not be able to see all the subtle energies around you, but you can learn to feel them, and soon you will find that information from the Universal Law has a way of jumping at you unexpectedly.

Events in your life gather energy as they come toward you, and you can feel that energy weeks and even years before they occur. Science will tell you it is not possible to foresee the future, and that is true for those who believe it to be so, but as you move out of the world's "group perception," feeling and even seeing the future will become second nature to you.

To harness the Universal Law effectively, you should watch its manifestation, which is basically every event in your life. Then link each event to your underlying feelings and attitudes. Realize that when things go well, it is solely because you put that image into the Universal Law and it responded. Imagine the Universal Law as a shipping clerk in a large mail-order company. He gets your order but has no idea who you are. If the order says "size 8," he sends out size 8. It is of no concern to him whether or not size 8 fits you. He merely complies with your request.

In daily life, your feelings, thoughts, and attitudes are your order form, so before you decide to change your present conditions, you will have to be very sure what you want from life. The Universal Law reacts spastically to uncertain messages. You have to write clearly, and you have to be ready to accept whatever you are looking for.

Let us say you want to win a large sum of money, give up your job, and spend the rest of your days lying in the sun. You dream about the cash, and you sigh and say, "Wouldn't it be lovely." But is that actually what you want? You might very soon find yourself bored, and though your mind would like to lounge in the sun, the inner you might say, "I should have stayed where I was; there was more potential there."

Creating energy for yourself through the Universal Law is not just a matter of

wishing for things, willy-nilly. You have to
realize that the power is within you, and
once you take the first step toward it, whatever you create will be for your highest
good. It might not be exactly what you
thought you wanted, but you had better be
ready for the consequences.

Before embarking on a miracle "action
plan," you ought to spend some time
meditating on the conditions or material
objects you want. The Universal Law is
the shipping clerk waiting for your clear
and concise order. The currency with
which you are going to pay for it is *belief*.

To create something with absolute cer-
tainty, you have to establish the feeling
within you that it has already happened—
that the condition you desire is already a
part of your life. This can be hard because
your mind, knowing nothing about the
workings of the Law, fights back.

You affirm, "I am rich," and your mind contradicts, "You're not." The conflict that develops confuses the Universal Law, which is about to deliver your heart's desire. This clash of opposing energies has been the challenge of the would-be initiate since the beginning of time. It is the hunt for the Grail, or the slaying of the dragon. It states that no one enters the kingdom of heaven within until he has tamed the dragon of negativity that he inherited from the collective unconscious. Figuratively, you will have to leave the earth plane even though you may still be very much a part of physical reality. Dimensions are not out there someplace between you and the stars; they are inner worlds or inner journeys.

These journeys have an inner reality and an outer manifestation in the physical, so anything you can conceive is actually a part of you right now. The fact that you do not have it on hand matters not. Whatever it is that you conceive is in a state of gradually becoming. If you affirm, "I am rich," you have to start feeling rich, thinking rich, and holding a rich attitude. Walk around expensive stores, have coffee in the best hotel in town, begin to act and feel as if you already have the vast fortune you know the Universal Law is about to deliver to you. In this way, you create a concrete reality of wealth within your inner journey, and it will become manifest in your outer journey, the physical world. If you can maintain that feeling and power and live as if your wish has already been granted by the Universal Law, your wish will be delivered, guaranteed.

But you cannot be halfhearted, or you will dissipate your personal power and nothing will happen. You have to take to the path like a warrior. You are going to achieve your goal. No matter what confronts you, no matter where you are right now, no matter what adversity you face, you will reach your objective. The Universal Law does not care whether you have your heart's desire or not. Therefore, you might as well make up your mind to collect.

You can have anything you want, and when you create it, it becomes yours. Often we feel we do not deserve success or wealth or complete health or anything else we might yearn for. We are taught in childhood that we are not worthy, or that somehow we owe something to society or the physical plane, or that we have some kind of special sin that we should atone for before we can enjoy what we want out of life.

This is not the case. The Law does not discriminate. It receives your energy and delivers diamonds or plain rocks, depend-

ing on what you put in. It is very important to look at the negative feelings you
have about yourself. It is easy to say, "Oh,
I never win anything," or "I am too old;
they will never hire me," or "I can never
be with that person; I am not pretty
enough." That kind of thinking is indica-
tive of the mind and its "logical" advice.

Miracles are not logical, so the last
thing you need is logical advice from the
mind. When such advice is given,
acknowledge the mind, thank it, and say,
"I do not accept any energy that is contrary to the unlimited power that lies
within me," then press on.

Infinite power is so magnanimous, so
powerful, so much more than the mind, that
it exists in a separate dimension, and that is
why the mind has difficulty perceiving that it
is even there. You will get an intuition or
feeling or a rush of excitement, but that is

all. You cannot really hear it, touch it, or taste it, but it comes 'round the mind like a breeze, and when it starts to work in your life, you will know it by the quality of the people and events that surround you.

Before we go to step four, the Miracle "Action Plan," let us briefly review some important points.

↶ The Universal Law, or Living Spirit, is unlimited. This force is within you. Therefore, what you are is also unlimited.

↶ The Universal Law is impartial and unemotional. It cannot discriminate. It will willingly give you anything you believe in.

↶ You are not your body or your emotions or your mind. You are a part of the Living Spirit, learning. No matter what your circumstances, the

Universal Law can be called upon at any time because it is the *real* you.

⌐ Whatever you create for yourself by understanding the mystical, meta-physical aspects of the Universal Law is yours—because you created it, you deserve it.

⌐ Miracles are not gifts from God; they are a part of what you are, which is God.

Finally, the Universal Law is in balance and harmony by its very nature. And so, as you set out on your "action plan," you will not be able to infringe on others. Whatever you create will have to be for yourself. You cannot will the Universal Law on to others, saying, "I want this to happen to my friend." This would be infringing, because, not knowing the nature of your friend's heroic life plan, you are not entitled to change it or in any way alter what he is going through at this time. He has to experience life for himself, as he also has unlimited power within him, and a part of his growth pattern is discovering that fact.

Within the Universal Law, there is no dual energy, good and bad, saints and sinners. There is just energy—one power that pervades all things, and everything is a part of the power. Differentiation between good and evil is just your perception, for within real energy there is no judgment. There is high energy and not-so-high energy, and at the end of this life you will have the opportunity to review what you have achieved, which will be a matter of how much you have succeeded in centering your life in a discipline of perceiving the Living Spirit and using it. But your review will not be emotional. You will be looking at the quality (or speed, if you like) of the energy you created. If you have harmed others, you have impeded your evolution by decelerating the life force within you. That is your karmic energy, and someday you will have to understand that it was not your highest path. But you cannot judge others, because, since the energy your mind perceives does not incorporate the nature of their heroic goal, you have no way of knowing that what they are going through is not exactly what they need karmically for their growth at this infinite point in their evolution.

There are no accidents or victims. Each person is responsible for his own evolution. Each pulls to himself the circumstances experienced in life. He puts in an order, so to speak, and gets back three cracked cups. That is a part of the learning pattern, trial and error.

This lifetime is yours. You may be involved in relationships and love others, but basically what you make of your life and how you pass through it is your evolution. We all learn to take responsibility for our own circumstances, and, within the Universal Law, we are not expected to take responsibility for the evolution of others. It might sound a bit harsh, but in the Law there is incredible clarity and justice.

That is why adversity is so useful. It allows people to look for something beyond day-to-day reality, and this brings them in touch with their true inner selves. In desperation, they begin to pull on their *unlimited power*, and they realize that anything can be changed, that suffering is a product of the inner self, and by looking at their inner selves, they can transform them. It has been said that there are no incurable diseases, only incurable people, and this is true of all energy within the Universal Law. Trying to fix your circumstances just physically or mentally will not work in the long run because deep-rooted inconsistencies will continue to surface in your life in various guises. To overcome something once and for all means going within yourself to discover the real causes of the disturbance.

This process or discovery will allow you more energy, which you can use to create the things you want in your life.

STEP FOUR ∽

The Miracle "Action Plan"

Write down on a piece of paper, in order of importance, the things and conditions you want. Do not let the mind "advise" you; it has limitations. Shoot for the moon, and be sure you leave nothing out. Chop and change your list until you are comfortable with it, but be clear about what you want. Use exact and precise wording to describe the conditions you require. Remember, the system works, so you must be definite in the way you describe your wants.

Here is what you do:

a) Read your list three times a day—once when you rise, once in the middle of the day, and once before bed.

b) Meditate on your miracles from time to time, and KNOW that the Universal Law has received your order and is just about to deliver.

c) Maintain silence. Talking about your miracles dissipates the energy drastically. Therefore, you cannot share your miracles with others until they happen.

d) Always act and think about your miracles as though you already have the conditions you desire.

e) Be open to the inner promptings of the unlimited power source as it instructs you in ways of getting what you want. Realize that the Universal Law has to deliver in the physical plane where you can make use of it. Your heart's desire can come from anywhere, so do not limit your field of expectation. Remain open and flexible at all times.

f) Smile a lot—the first miracle is on its way!

∽ ∽ ∽

Understanding Energy

Since the mind has no way of knowing how the Universal Law is going to deliver your miracle, do not waste time trying to figure it out, just KNOW. Your thoughts should be like acorns that develop gradually into oaks; if you dig them up to discover how things are going, your tree will perish. It is important to avoid fretting. Center on the feeling that some way, somehow, the Universal Law will not let you down, because everything in the universe is energy.

Solid objects appear as such only because their atoms and molecules move at high speed. In fact, reality is both solid and not solid at the same time, and this applies to thought-forms. They are real and even more powerful than physical reality because they are not constrained by the limits of the material plane. But you cannot take them apart and analyze them. You have to create them and let them fly.

Then through enthusiasm and belief, you energize the Universal Law and encourage it to deliver. Try at all times to keep your thoughts pure and on target. If doubt creeps in, do not allow it to dominate for long. Look at doubt from above yourself. Realize that it is just the mind fretting, not understanding, creating objections through ignorance, and whatever you have set in motion will happen.

As you work with the power, it will have a way of showing you the next move at every turn. Believe in it. Know that this inner force is so powerful that it will pull you into excitement and adventure beyond your dreams. Keep it pure, remain silent, and remember to keep your methods secret.

Everything that surrounds you has the Living Spirit within it in varying degrees. Living things express it more than do inanimate objects, but all have it. The more you come into contact with the Universal Law within you, the more you are in touch with things around you. Everything becomes a symbol and strength to you. The world helps you, and the fuller you become, the more dimensions you can pull from.

A very dear friend was walking along a street one day wondering what to do with her life. She was at a crossroads literally and figuratively. Life was flat. She craved inspiration and had asked the Universal Law to direct her. As she stepped from the curb, a passing car nearly knocked her over, and as it screeched round the corner, a book fell out of its trunk.

It was a book about man's quest for the Universal Power, and it changed her life. Shortly, she left that town and embarked on a whole new evolutionary path that, over a period of time, has taken her to great metaphysical heights and into countries and relationships she could not have conceived of before.

The Universal Law provided her with a special teaching in the form of that book, and she, being in tune, was ready to benefit. And so it should for you. As you work toward your miracle, watch for every sign, for every change around you, and you will see the Universal Law communicating

with you. The more you trust it, the more
the energy is encouraged to reveal itself,
and various unusual things begin to occur.
Your energy quickens, and opportunities
pop up like corks on a lake. Then you will
KNOW that the power is truly with you.

This coming in tune, more than anything
else, will help you manifest your desires. You
cannot act negatively in one part of the Universal Law and expect the other part to
deliver your miracles unaffected. As you
watch your life, you become expert at read-
ing symbols, and you see that you are the
only one responsible for what you are and
that everything around you expresses an
energy. The clothes you wear, the things you
say, the people you associate with, the foods
you eat, and the places you go are all statements to the Universal Law of what you are.

The quality of these statements, or the
coming in tune with yourself and your

surroundings, is the key to your spiritual unfoldment. What you are has great power. Its energy oscillates and reflects the amount of Living Spirit or God-Force that you express. The more you work on your life, the more you accept responsibility, the more energy you will have, and the greater will be your expectations.

Suppose you have a special project in mind and you want to be sure that you have the maximum possible energy available. Let us say you are heading for a job interview. You have put the job on your miracle list, the Universal Law has opened a door, and you are halfway there! Here is what you do:

1) Continue to see your miracle coming into physical reality. See yourself with the job granted until 72 hours before the interview, then forget about it.

2) On the day of your interview, rise early. Spend as much time as possible on your own. Avoid interpersonal conflicts. Tell the Universal Law that you are ready and willing to accept the miracle you have been asking for.

3) Abstain from such energy-lowering substances as alcohol and drugs.

4) Eat lightly. The Universal Law manifests *in* you and *through* you. If you eat great amounts of heavy food, your energy slows, and the Universal Law within you has difficulty expressing itself. You should have salads, fruit, natural healthy food, in sparing quantities. Stay away from junk food.

5) Before you set off for your interview, relax a moment. See the situation as flowing and positive. If you
   already know the person you will be
   meeting, see him or her in your
   mind's eye, happy and smiling,
   receptive to your energy. See the
   interview going well; see the miracle delivered.

STEP SIX ∽

Understanding Time

Within the Universal Law, there is no time. Things are in a state of gradual evolvement. A tree has no concept of time because its essence is eternal. It responds to the warmth of the sun, but it is not "in time." It develops from seed, expanding gradually to full maturity, and so it is with the Universal Law. It can deliver instantly, but if your energy is not all there, it will seem to you as if it has taken time. You have to learn patience and keep moving toward your goal, knowing that your thought-form will be manifest.

If you are moving toward one particular miracle, and a different avenue opens unexpectedly, take it. The Universal Law delivers in strange ways, and what you think you desire may just be your way of expressing a totally different goal.

A good friend of mine wanted more than anything else to be a film director. He graduated from film school in London but found that he could not get any work because of a technical complication. To work in films in England at that time, you had to have a union card. But you could not get a union card unless you were working. In effect, the union created a "closed shop." My friend's miracle was stuck!

One day, out of the blue, he bumped into an old school friend who owned a restaurant, and due to his financial straits, he gladly accepted a job as a waiter. Working hard each day, he spent his spare time watching films and keeping his dream alive through study. Each day at noon, a well-dressed old man came into the restaurant. My friend served him diligently, and over the months the two of them became friends. One day my friend asked the old man what he did for a living. The old man replied that he was just about to retire from a job he had held for many years.

"What job is that?" asked my friend. "Oh! It's pretty boring, really," replied the old man, "I am president of the filmmaker union...not much ever happens."

Fifteen years later, I was flying across the United States, lazily watching an "in flight" movie when, to my great delight, I saw my friend's name on the credits of a major film. His miracle had been delivered.

When you move into an energy alignment, you can never tell what will happen. Watch for signs, use your feelings to help you decide, and if, after that, you are still not sure, do NOTHING.

If a direction is right, you will know it automatically. If, however, making up your mind requires you to go through great trials and tribulations, you can be sure that that particular course is not the one for you. Basically, it is well to remember that if you have to ponder a decision, it is usually a mistake. When the Universal Law delivers, you will know.

Start your miracle list with a couple of modest requests. Then, as you experience the Universal Law delivering, you will feel the power of success around you, and that in itself becomes a valuable affirmation. Each time you reorganize your list, spend a few moments thinking about how well your last miracles worked. Affirm your power by visualizing your success; then, as you accomplish one miracle after another, you will have the confidence to go to other things.

∽∽∽∾

Understanding Your Personal Power

In conclusion, we will discuss how to establish an energy of power around you. Your mind's natural negative alignment will tend to make you think that your miracles are not going to come true. Therefore, in order to achieve complete success, you have to work constantly on your mind's doubt. Remind yourself that you are not your mind and you do not accept any energy contrary to your goals. In this way, you establish a pattern of positive affirmation in your life.

Write down in your own words nine affirmations that express your belief in yourself and your complete fulfillment in this lifetime. Three affirmations for the dawn, three for the day, and three for the night. Before reviewing your miracle list, relax, center your mind, then read your affirmations slowly. Make your affirmations strong, be sure that you feel their power and that they mean something special to you. The words and feelings that *you* believe in have the strongest energy. Here are a few examples from which you can build:

↪ I AM A POWERFUL, POSITIVE INDI-
   VIDUAL, AND ALL EVENTS IN THIS
   DAY ARE FOR MY HIGHEST GOOD.

↪ WHAT I AM IS BEAUTIFUL, AND
   I PULL TO ME THIS DAY ONLY
   BEAUTY AND REFRESHMENT.

∽ THIS DAY IS A DAY OF BALANCE.
I AM COMPLETELY AWARE OF MY
BODY AND ALL ITS NEEDS.

∽ WHAT I AM IS ETERNAL, IMMORTAL,
UNIVERSAL, AND INFINITE. I SEE
ONLY BEAUTY AND STRENGTH
EVERY MOMENT OF MY LIFE.

∽ I SEE ONLY BEAUTY IN ALL THE
PEOPLE WHO ARE PULLED TO ME,
AND WHAT I AM STRENGTHENS
AND REFRESHES WHAT THEY ARE.

∽ WHAT I AM IS INFINITE. I DO NOT
JUDGE THE EVOLUTION OF
OTHERS. WHAT THEY ARE RIGHT
NOW IS FOR THEIR HIGHEST GOOD.

∽ EACH ACTION I TAKE THIS DAY
IS AN EXPRESSION OF THE GOD-
FORCE. THEREFORE, EACH
ACTION I TAKE IS A PART OF MY
INFINITE CREATIVITY.

↪ THERE IS NO REAL SIN, ONLY
   ENERGY. I FOLLOW THE ENERGY
   OF MY HIGHEST EVOLUTION AT
   ALL TIMES, AND SO BE IT.

↪ I AM OPEN AT ALL TIMES TO
   COMMUNICATION FROM MY
   INNER SELF, AND THAT COM-
   MUNICATION LEADS ME TO MY
   HIGHEST EVOLUTION.

↪ I GIVE THANKS FOR THE BEAUTY
   OF THIS DAY, AND MAY THE
   ENERGY OF THIS NIGHT BRING RE-
   BUILDING AND RE-VIEW. SO BE IT.

Your affirmations act like small twigs in
a fire. As you arise, you begin to build energy in the day. Use your affirmations to keep
that energy going. Center for a moment to
acknowledge your infinite beauty and your
place in all things, then proceed.

If you are pulled into interpersonal conflict, take a few minutes on your own to repair your energy, and before going out into the day, be sure that your energy is strong. If you care for your power and you balance and center your life, no harm can befall you, and you enter into worlds that few people are even aware of.

Create your day the way you want it; see it going well; see each person you meet as positive and open to your energy; see the day as harmonious and flowing; and see yourself evolving through each and every experience.

Finally, before setting out into the day, see the white light of the Living Spirit around you, protecting you and strengthening what you are. Realize that the more you believe in yourself, the stronger the white light becomes. It acts as your shield, and from time to time each day you should reenergize it by seeing it vibrant and strong, and by affirming that what you are is a part of the Living Spirit, or God, and that each moment of your life is one of exhilaration and learning.

Your position on the earth plane as a miracle-maker is inherent in the infinite power that lies within you. That limitless source lies there waiting for you to step up and collect your heritage, and when you do, the power will always be with you...

...and that is guaranteed. So be it.

᠔᠔᠔

About the Author

Author and lecturer Stuart Wilde is one of the real characters of the self-help, human potential movement. His style is humorous, controversial, poignant, and transformational. He has written 14 books, including the very successful Taos Quintet, which are considered classics in their genre. They are: *Miracles, Affirmations, The Force, The Quickening*, and *The Trick to Money Is Having Some*. Stuart's books have been translated into 12 languages.

∾ ∾ ∾

STUART WILDE
INTERNATIONAL TOUR AND
SEMINAR INFORMATION

For information on Stuart Wilde's latest tour
and seminar dates in the USA and
Canada, contact:

White Dove International
P.O. Box 1000
Taos, NM 87571
(505) 758-0500 (phone)
(505) 758-2265 (fax)

Stuart's Website:
powersource.com/wilde

～

We hope you enjoyed this Hay House book.
If you would like to receive a free catalog
featuring additional Hay House books and
products, or if you would like information
about the Hay Foundation,
please write to:

Hay House, Inc.
P.O. Box 5100
Carlsobad, CA 92018-5100
(760) 431-7695 or **(800) 654-5126**
(760) 431-6948 (fax) or **(800) 650-5115 (fax)**

Please visit the Hay House Website at:
hayhouse.com

～